Monetize Your Message

The Training and Internet Marketing Mashup That Will Transform Your Message into a Publishing Powerhouse

J. Scott MacMillan

Monetize Your Message

Copyright © 2016 by J. Scott MacMillan

Forward

It's an incredibly exciting time to be an entrepreneur. Just consider these statistics for a moment: Every year, $33 billion is spent in the corporate training and e-learning industry, $27 billion is spent in the e-book and online publishing industry, $17 billion in the mobile app market and $1.3 billion is spent in coaching industries.

In other words, right now, opportunity is everywhere. Combine that with the rapid advances we're continually making in technology that make it not only possible, but simple to work from anywhere, distribute content across myriad platforms with the click of a single button and connect with new people around the globe.

J. Scott MacMillan and I followed a parallel path as we shaped our careers. We both started out in a corporate environment, and we both chose to take advantage of the immense opportunity in the marketplace to go out on our own and start our own businesses.

Leaving my corporate job to start my own company wasn't the easiest thing I did, but it was one of the most rewarding. There have been some big wins, some sleepless nights, some periods of uncertainty and some bucket list dreams that my business has made come true, including a family vacation in which I actually earned revenue while I was showing my two young boys the wonders of the state of California.

In starting my own business, what I learned above all is that you need a system, a proven plan. That's why Scott's *Monetize Your Message* system is such a powerful tool for any business owner—or any aspiring business owner with a message to share. (You know who you are!) What I love about his model is that it combines the best of the two worlds—corporate training and Internet marketing techniques—into one comprehensive system. There's so much power in this synergy. It's one I've used many times over both in my business, and with my clients to help them produce a new level of results. I know it's going to be a difference-maker in your business.

The other element that's so powerful about Scott's system is that he not only gives you the *why*, the overall system, but he also gives you the *how*. I can't tell you how many times I've invested in a book or a training system that seemed revolutionary, only to discover that there was no substance behind the excitement. There was no map to actually get me from where I was to where I wanted to be.

Scott's five-step approach will give you that map. By the end of the program, you'll have all the tools you need to build a successful business by marketing and selling your unique message through online courses and products. He also lays out, step by step, the fundamental strategies that have made Internet marketing so successful—and he'll share them with you in enough detail that you'll be able to implement these sophisticated strategies even if you're not "tech savvy." I know I didn't know what a lead magnet and a tripwire were when I first got into the business, and I was grateful to my mentors for laying everything out for me. Scott will do the same for you. And even if you've been in the business for a while, I know you'll still learn something from Scott's system that will make a meaningful difference in the way you're marketing your business and your message.

Finally, throughout his book, Scott emphasizes something that's near and dear to my heart: the need for a standard of *quality* content. The Internet has given us the ability to publish an eBook in a few hours or to push out a blog post to the world within seconds. However, along with that capacity for lightning-quick delivery comes the temptation to put out content that's less than perfect. During the days when print was still king, we would obsess over every comma, every adjective and even every adverb to make sure our finished product would pass muster for years to come.

While I'm not advocating a return to what feels now like the Stone Age, I am echoing what Scott suggests in *Monetize Your Message*: We must continually raise our standards and create the highest quality content and products we're capable of producing. A commitment to quality will not only set you apart from the other fly-by-night operations that inevitably crop up on the Internet, but it will also help you move ahead of most of your competitors in your industry, giving you a distinct advantage. And, finally, when you're in front of a prospect, up on stage in front of an audience or live on a webinar asking your future customers to invest in you, the quality of your product will give you a new level of courage to take that leap of faith and ask for the sale.

You have inside you a unique mix of experience, knowledge and expertise that no one else has. Maybe you've discovered, as Scott says, your burning message that the world needs to hear. Whatever you're ready to share with the world, Scott's *Monetize Your Message* is the system you need to get yourself heard and build the foundation for a solid, enduring business that will show you new levels of freedom, excitement, confidence and joy.

Enjoy Scott's book—and as you build your business, remember to enjoy not just your successes, but also the journey.

- Pam Hendrickson
  Best-selling author and product creator

About The Author:

I started my career as a systems engineer with a Fortune 100 company. I loved learning everything I could about engineering. This was necessary as I graduated from college with a Psychology degree. I was able to perform at a high-level so long as I had a willingness to learn new skills and apply them. I loved learning so much that I moved into corporate training and development; I studied advanced adult learning theory and many instructional design methods to teach adults everything from how to make and install equipment to how to sell it. Even though I loved my corporate career, I was one of those people who always had a burning desire to own my own business.

When an opportunity presented itself, I decided it was time to give my dream a shot. I left my corporate job to start my own business. I morphed all my passions into an Internet marketing business, and helped many businesses ditch the Yellow Pages and start making a profit.

With my corporate training background and Internet marketing business, I started helping people take their core message and create online courses and information products to sell via the Internet.

Just like any good information product entrepreneur with a message, I have put my 20 plus years of training and development experience and my unique life experiences into this book. I have successfully blended adult learning theory, which is heavily used in corporate America, with fresh Internet marketing and personal development concepts in order to build a system that can help anyone with a message to create a successful online information business.

- Happy learning, J. Scott

Table Of Contents

This book is for you if…:

- You have a burning message that the world needs to hear.

- You love helping other people.

- You are an author or speaker trying to make money on your books or speaking gigs alone.

- You are a life coach trying to make money through one-on-one sessions and you would love to find a way to earn a living without being tied down to so many sessions.

- You own or run a small business that is looking for a way to attract additional customers, who will trust you and therefore open their wallets and buy from you.

- You run a corporate marketing department and you would like a fresh way to communicate your message to potential customers.

- Maybe you are none of the above, but you have a burning message that is dying to be heard, and you are not sure why anyone would listen to you.

- You want to make and extra $1,000, $5,000 even $10,000 a month.

- You want to help as many people as you can and make a difference in the world.

Welcome to you all. You are in the right place.

You all might be saying, *Yes I would like to make more money and help a lot of people, but why would anyone want to listen to me?* My answer is: *Why not you?!*

Look, everything you can think of has already been thought of, documented, and is available on the Internet. Did you know that every minute, 2.4 billion messages are posted on Facebook and users post 277 thousand tweets? Guess how many hours of video are uploaded onto YouTube every minute? Seventy-two and a lot of this minute-by-minute data influx is junk. But there is no one else on the planet exactly like you and you have a unique perspective, and if you can articulate and convey that view to people, you will connect with others who value that view. Next thing you know, you have a customer. And where there is one on the Internet, there are millions.

In this book, I will present a compelling case which suggests that you can create a successful business based on your message by creating online courses and supporting information products, and marketing and selling them through the Internet.

I will introduce you to a unique 5-phase system based on the mashup of traditional corporate training concepts, including adult learning models, and current Internet marketing strategies that you can use to create your platform, marketing funnel, and online courses. This will help you to market and launch your ideas to the world and make money while you sleep.

By the end of this journey, you will have created a business built on your passion and fashioned around the life you have always dreamed of.

If you are just starting out and don't have a website, Facebook page, or have not written a thing, or If you just have a great idea or message, or you are an expert in an area and you want to capitalize on it, then you should follow this system from the beginning to the end. It will offer you the best chance to succeed. Together, we will help many people through your message; you will also make some money while you sleep.

If you have not already done so, please sign up for the bonus videos. They will enhance your experience of this book, as they will enable you to dive deeper into various concepts that we will cover.

Visit http://monetizeyourmessagetoday.com/bookcta to access the bonus videos and exercises.

Are You On-Board?

We live in a world that is more connected, and where people are more educated and aware of their neighbors, either down the road or across the globe, then at anytime in history. Technology and the Internet have cascaded us into an information extravaganza. With a click of a button, you can communicate with more than 80% of the planet. These technologies raise the quality of life for almost every person on the planet by providing education and instant communication. What does this mean for entrepreneurs? For starters, more resources and technologies are available to convey your message and sell your products to the masses; also, they are amazingly cheap, if not free.   Individuals and businesses can consume your message on billions of computers, smartphones, tablets, and even televisions.

At no other time in history can anyone who has an idea, a message, or a theory, disseminate information to the masses as easily. The barrier to entry is extremely low which compels you to take advantage of this phenomenon and shout your message to the world.

As for the market potential, did you know that the e-learning industry will generate revenues of $51.5 billion by 2016? Ebook sales will reach $7.9 billion by 2016 and the trend just keeps increasing. So, there's a voracious appetite for online learning, which makes it an ideal time to start an online information business.

"Okay, that sounds fine" I hear you saying, "but how can I make a living by shouting my message to the world"? Well, keep reading, as you will learn how to create, publish, and make money with your message - while you're sleeping (which is a pretty cool bonus).

The four main concepts required to develop a successful online information business are as follows:

1. Great content that adds value and makes people know, like, and trust you
2. Structured and systematic creation & distribution of content
3. Unrelenting follow-up
4. Understanding & solving your customer's pain

If you nail these four concepts, you will have a very successful online information business.

We will cover these four concepts in detail and see exactly how they're created and implemented. We'll cover a five-phase process that systematically tackles each of the concepts, and uses the power of the online course to achieve them. I learned this basic format while working as an instructional designer in corporate training development and through managing my Internet marketing business and dealing with customers. It has served me well in creating multiple online information businesses. It will also serve you well.

The system you are about to learn uses a combination of basic adult learning theory and Internet marketing. While working as a corporate instructional designer, I followed the ADDIE model. It was originally created by Florida State University as a model to explain the processes involved in the formulation of an instructional systems development program that would train individuals to perform a particular job. The model can be applied to any curriculum. The model contains five phases: analyze, design, develop, implement, and evaluate. The original idea was to complete each phase before moving on to the next. Over the years, the model has become more dynamic and interactive. By combining this model with successful Internet marketing concepts, I have developed a system that takes its roots from the basic ADDIE model; however, it is extremely fluid and adaptable to today's rapid pace of information adoption methods, such as social media and email marketing. I call it the Monetize Your Message (MYM) system. The MYM system is the foundation of this book and I will explain the entire system. There are, of course, many different methods and systems which talk about online courses and information products. The MYM system is unique because it incorporates both traditional corporate training concepts, such as adult learning theories, and current Internet marketing techniques into one comprehensive system. Other programs talk a lot about theories and concepts; however, I will not only cover the basic concepts of creating an online information business and instructional design concepts, but I'll show you exactly how I do it. While I will discuss several tool options, for the most part I will teach you the MYM system way of doing things. You will either adopt it and be very successful or you won't, but I want you to know up front that if you follow the MYM system in its entirety, you will have the best chance of creating a very successful online information business.

The nice thing about being an entrepreneur and creating an online information business is that you have the chance to choose what's in or out, not your boss, stockholders, or other investors. You have the final word: it's your business and your message. People will respond positively and will want more from you.

It's up to you to do your research and put in the hard work necessary to make sure they like your message. As you will learn, your chances of doing that are greater if you take the time to really understand your customers and find out what their pains are, and then create products that teach them how to solve those problems. That's the key to this business.

Before I outline the concepts in this book, a word about outsourcing. Building this business has lots of moving parts and you'll need to keep track of them all. I'll show you how to do that and let you know what areas are okay and even preferable to outsource. You won't be able to do everything yourself though. I know some of you will try, and that's up to you, but delegating some tasks will not only help you to maintain your sanity but might just make your final products look a bit more professional.

There are definitely areas you don't want to outsource though. You will certainly need to undertake the analyze phase on your own or with your partners. Some of this involves personal stuff that has to come from your heart and your head, as this will ensure you create a successful business.

Online Information Business Vs. Content Marketing

The MYM system can be used to create a complete online information business or to create and implement a content marketing strategy. In either case, the system follows a traditional instructional design process and includes the five phases of the ADDIE model and successful Internet marketing strategies. This content marketing strategy is built using the 5 phases minus the online course. I'll cover the entire online information business portion first and then point out where things might differ if you want to only focus on content marketing. If you follow the entire system, you might even want to use it to meet your training requirements.

Book Overview

During the **analyze phase,** you will dive deep into your life perspective and define your reasons for wanting to convey your message to the world. This journey is a blast but it's not for the faint of heart. You will need to really understand why you want to jump on this rocket blaster of a business.

After you figure out why you want to convey your message to the world, you'll brainstorm what your products will be for the next two years. You'll dive deep into client analysis so you understand who your customers are and what their pain is. After you complete this task, you will know your customer better than yourself, which is critical to creating a successful online information business. Next, you perform some external business analysis where you will determine who your competitors are and what they are doing to gain the attention of the customers you want. Finally, you will start to design your branding and online platform, such as your website/blog and social media sites. What's a platform you say? It's simply the stage where you house and distribute your free content and branding. Before anyone will pay attention to you and ultimately buy from you, they need to know, like, and trust you. You've probably heard that before. It's a staple of any business to encourage customers to buy from them. Few people buy from people they don't like or trust, and if they do, they're usually unhappy about it and will not buy from them again. This is a critical step in developing a successful online information business, however, a lot people either skip it or do not pay it enough attention. With the MYM system, before you put anything out for customers to buy, you first need to publish a lot of free content in order to encourage people to know, like, and trust you.

During the **design phase,** you will start to sketch out what your online course will look like and what type of content you will use. You will create a design document, which will be your bible for the rest of the project. At the completion of this phase, you will have a working blueprint of your entire online information business.

Once all the design work is finished, you will start on the **develop phase**. Here you will actually begin to assemble the content for your online course and marketing funnel assets so you can make some money while you're sleeping. This is the really fun part. You'll learn all the ins and outs of what I have learned through my years of working in corporate training development and Internet marketing. By the end of the develop stage, you will have completed your online course and marketing funnel assets and be ready to launch your online course.

The **implement phase** is where you finally get to make some money. This is where you will create a sales and marketing funnel and launch your online course.

One area where many online information businesses fail is the marketing of their platform and products. Successful information businesses consist of 10% creation and 90% marketing. If you're not ready for that, then you might want to turn back because without a strong marketing and implementation plan, you will not be successful. This includes creating sales and marketing funnels, a launch strategy, and various methods to increase traffic.

The last phase is the **evaluate phase.** You'll learn how to take all of that momentum you built during your launch and capitalize on it to create long-lasting relationships with your customers; this way they will keep coming back for more. You will obtain feedback from your customers in order to make improvements for your next launch. You will prepare for the next steps in your journey, and decide if you're ready for high ticket group sessions or live events that really bring in the money.

Whew, that's a lot but we're going to have a blast. How often do you get to absorb yourself in your life's work? This will be challenging but fun and extremely rewarding - not to mention profitable - even while your sleeping.

So, are you coming aboard this rocket ship? If you've read this far, I bet your bouncing up and down with excitement to get going. So let's dive right in.

Visit http://monetizeyourmessagetoday.com/bookcta to access bonus videos and exercises.

The Ultimate Mashup

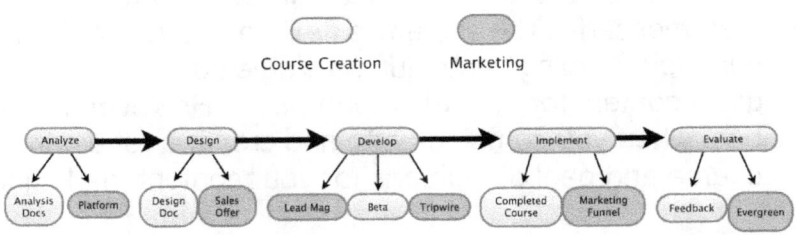

MYM is based on the 5 phases of the ADDIE model used in corporate training. Each phase builds on the last, can overlap, and have both course creation and marketing outflows.

As previously mentioned, I started my career as a systems engineer and quickly moved into corporate training and development. The combination of these two disciplines allowed me to understand the demands of a learner and the responsibilities of a trainer to make sure the learner comes out of training with the ability to perform their job at a high level. During my 20 years in training and development, I studied many adult learning theories and instructional design systems to ensure that learners were properly and efficiently trained within the corporate training budget. When I left the corporate setting and started working with small businesses, I was mainly helping them to attract new customers through content marketing and getting people to know, like, and trust them. I used the techniques I learned as an instructional designer to help them create quality marketing content. I combined this with tried and true Internet marketing strategies and came up with the MYM system. I soon realized that the same system also worked great for authors, speakers, and coaches who were struggling to convey their message to the masses and create a viable business. The mashup of the systematic approach to creating training lends itself perfectly to creating high quality content that can be used for any business who wants to attract customers with their message. The system is flexible enough to create a complete training curriculum, a single course, or just great content for marketing purposes. However, it works best when you combine both, and create a robust training course and peel off portions for your content marketing.

One of the reasons that following the entire MYM system is so powerful is that the rigor of following the ADDIE model ensures that you have fully analyzed and systematically created an online course and associated products that address your customers' pain. Each phase has many tasks that output to multiple outflow documents, which aid in course development and marketing.

Rest assured that when using this structured approach to deliver your message, it will encourage people to know, like, and trust you as well as solve their problems and enhance their lives.

Why Online Courses?

With all the different types of information products, why do I focus on online courses? One of the main reasons is that no other medium is as diverse and robust as online courses. Not only can you appeal to structured learners that like to read to absorb information, you can also use graphics and video to appeal to visual and auditory learners through the same delivery vehicle. Video is another reason I advocate for online courses. No other media can deliver the learning experience like a video. It stimulates both hemispheres of the brain effecting both hearing and sight senses. Videos can also be very expressive and build on emotions, which reinforce learning. You can also charge a lot more for online courses versus other mediums, especially if you include live webinars where customers have access to the expert.

Remember to visit http://monetizeyourmessagetoday.com/bookcta to access bonus videos and exercises.

Analyze Phase

During the analyze phase, you will clarify problems, define goals and objectives, and collect necessary data.

The first step is to spend some time defining and reflecting on your life perspective so you understand why you are creating this business. You will then define your goals and objectives and find out who your customers and competitors are. You'll also brainstorm the online course you want to create as well as the associated information products and develop a timeframe. Finally, you will start to create your platform. Sometimes analysis isn't fun, but if you follow through with this phase, you will reap the benefits down the road. Since you will be collecting a lot of information, it's a good idea to come up with a data collection method. I like to use bulleted lists created in a word processor like **Microsoft Word** or **Apple Pages**. A spreadsheet will also work fine.

Just make sure you can easily refer to the data when you are designing and developing your online course.

If you're a business only wanting to create a content marketing strategy, then you may skip the life perspective analysis and move directly into the business analysis component. On the other hand, it wouldn't hurt to go through the life perspective analysis by substituting your organization for an individual as it may help you define why you are creating a content marketing strategy in the first place. You may also skip the last step of the process, which involves creating a platform. If you're a business that's been around for any length of time, you will surely have at least some of the platforms we'll talk about; however, if you don't, then feel free to use this method to create them.

Life Perspective

Remember when I said that you will experience ups and downs in this business? There will be times when you will wonder why you decided to take on this adventure. That's why you need a solid life perspective on why and who you are doing this for. This is a creative process and things will change as you proceed, but you must start with a clear vision and well-defined reasons.

Start off by listing your financial goals; determine how much money you want to make with this business. Is it a side business that brings in some extra cash or will this business sustain your family and put your kids through college? To start with, jot down some monthly or yearly figures.

Here is one of the biggest questions you'll need to answer. Why is this business important to you? Who will you help with the money you make? This business is about creating a platform for what you want to do personally and professionally. Think about where you want to be in the next five or ten years. How do you want to spend your time? Do you want to travel or stay home and garden? What do you want to create? What is your ultimate vision for your future? Also, define how you think your online information business, created from your life's passion or message, can get you there and how long it will take.

This is what you'll think about when you're trying to edit a blog article at midnight or create a video after 15 takes.

For me it's about having freedom. Freedom to work on the things I enjoy doing and the freedom to decide when to work on them. I like to work off and on during the evening so I can sleep in a bit and take my time in the morning.

It's also about having time to spend with my children and provide for them. They're both in college now, so freedom to be able to drive to their campus for the day to hang with them is very important to me. The other day, I decided I needed some kid time, so I texted them and said "Kids, clear your calendar, I'm coming down to hang out." We had a wonderful day and I was so grateful that I have a business created around the things that are important to me.

While freedom is important for me, a friend of mine loves speaking and traveling and being on the road as much as possible; therefore, her business is set up around being flexible enough so she can travel extensively. She actually just sold everything she had to travel the world and work wherever there is WiFi.

When you complete this exercise, you will have a clear vision. Only then will you be ready to start creating your business.

Business Analysis

Portfolio Analysis

Now that you have your life perspective defined, it's time to **brainstorm your online course**. Don't think that just because you are thinking about your online course that you are going to create content for it yet. You have a lot of work to do before you do that, but it's good to have a solid idea about your online course before you start building your business. Basically your business will be built around the concept of your online course. You will be breaking it into smaller products that will act as stand alone marketing funnel assets or information products. In other words, you will be creating mini versions of your online course and using them to encourage your customers to take actions that move them closer to buying from you, such as giving you their email address. We call these **micro-commitments.** The more micro-commitments your customers perform, the more likely they are to buy from you.

Once you have your online course identified, it's time to brainstorm more products and events. This is the time to let go and dream. If you charge $397 for your first online course then maybe you'll want to charge $499 to $1027 for your next product. Maybe you could organize a live event where people will travel around the globe to work with you. That's very possible and should be part of smart business planning. By thinking about a full product portfolio now, it helps you think of your business as a real money making entity, not just a one-time website with only one product to offer. Remember, we are building a business here.

 For example, if you have an online course about how to attract more customer reviews for your business it could consist of seven modules with five videos per module and downloadable PDF worksheets to help them work through the process. You could also throw in Photoshop templates of postcards they could give to their customers asking them to write a review. You could also include sample emails they could use to send to their customers asking for reviews. You could also throw in a few bonuses like pre-recorded webinars on the customer review process. I'm listing these items to give you an idea about creating standard online courses. If you have any content already created or partially created, list them also.

Subsequently, describe the strengths and weaknesses of your online information business. Finally, brainstorm what you want to create within the next 12-24 months. This can be a combination of your online course and a follow-up event or maybe a book and an online course. This is just to get you started; you will be building a more formal project plan and design document later.

Next, you'll switch gears just a bit and start on the next part of the business analysis phase. This is where you will identify your target customers and their pains, as well as your competitors.

Good business analysis is essential to any successful business endeavor. Without it, you're shooting at a target blindfolded. I know there are some that like to shoot first and aim later, but that approach usually doesn't keep the money rolling in.

Before you build your online information business, you will spend time analyzing what **niche** you want to be in or are in, who your **competitors** are, and what **channels** or platforms they are using to reach their customers, i.e., Facebook, Youtube, etc. Then you will spend considerable time analyzing and defining who your **clients** are. This may be the most critical step in the entire process and failure to nail this one is the cause of many business failures. You will round out the business analysis with some basic **SEO and traffic analysis** so that you have an idea of where your customers are hanging out and what you need to do to attract their attention. Finally, once you have a good idea of where you are heading, it's time to estimate a **budget** to get this business off the ground.

Niche Analysis:

Before you analyze your competitors and clients, you need to understand your broader niche. You probably already know what it is, so just jot it down. If you don't know, then start with a few key words you think would describe what your message is about and do a Google search. Do some research and you might discover that you are in the "underwater basket weaving" niche. You don't need to spend too much time on this, but it's helpful to identify your niche when you're establishing your marketing plan.

Client Analysis:

Remember, the fourth concept that must be fulfilled in order to create a successful online information business is: **solve your customer's pain**. You need to know your customer inside and out. You can achieve this with a client analysis.

First, find out and detail who your customers are. Try to narrow your focus down to the one person who will benefit most from your products. Trying to be everything to everyone spells disaster for businesses.

It's a good idea to create a basic profile of your best customer. Write down their gender, age, profession, income level, background, and life circumstances. Even write down a physical description of them. Doing this allows you to write your content as if you were speaking to this one person. It also makes your content resonate with your audience and brings a warmness that will ensure you continue to attract the right customers to your business.

Now, to really understand your customers' pain, answer the following questions. These insightful questions have been adapted from Pam Hendrickson and Mike Koenigs' wonderful program: "Make, Market, Launch It."

- If they could snap their fingers and make three life changes happen immediately, what would they be?
- What are their three biggest frustrations?
- What is their single biggest fear?
- What is the conversation inside their head? What do they say to themselves about the problems they have?

- What is their perspective on their life? From that perspective, how do they perceive you?
- What must they believe about you and your product or service to buy from you?
- What myths do they currently have about your product or service that you will shatter?
- What core objections do they have about your product or service that would cause them not to buy from you?

There are many ways you can answer the above questions. You can start by hanging out with your potential customers at networking events or live training events that target your niche. While networking, ask them some of these questions. You can also hang out on social media sites in your niche. Join relevant forums and start reading, asking questions, and commenting on topics. Find popular magazines in your niche to understand your potential customers. You can survey your audience by asking questions on your social media platforms or email list. In the next section, we will cover competitive analysis, which allows you to find out what marketing messages your competitors are using to solve their customers' pain. However you can, find ways to validate the answers to the above questions, as this will give you a good understanding of your customer and their pains.

This analysis will be very useful for your online information business. Getting a good handle on this is actually a make or break area for your business. Take it that seriously.

One of my clients, we'll call him Larry, didn't understand this when he created his first information product. He didn't spend as much time as he should have on his client analysis. He was so eager to convey his message that he dove right in and began creating content. Only after he had created all the videos, exercises, and content did he realize that his audience was not going to invest in this type of information product. He was targeting small businesses with an online course on how to attain more online reviews and build a business around a five-star reputation. The content was good and the practice was solid but small brick and mortar businesses have a million things to worry about and they don't have the time or the money to buy an information product, even if it would help their business. Had he undertaken better client analysis at the beginning of his project, he would have known this and come up with another plan. After we worked on his client analysis, he decided to offer a reputation service along with his training so that busy small business owners could use his system to automatically gather customer reviews.

Competitive Analysis:

Next, you will define who your competitors are by doing a competitive analysis. This includes:

- Gaining an insight into the types of content being produced by your competitors
- Understanding the marketing techniques that are bringing them success
- Performing a breakdown of the social landscape, including the types of content being shared as well as the people who are engaging with it

Here are a few tools that can help with your competitive analysis:
- **Follow.net and Similarweb.com** - These tools give you information on your competition including their online marketing strategies.

- **Facebook Insights** - Demographics regarding the people you will be targeting with your ads.
- **Reddit** - Forums that host conversations about your clients' needs.
- **Amazon and Kindle** - Find out if there are books on your niche to see who your competitors might be.

Competitive analysis is important because if you can find out who is already resonating with your potential customers, you can piggyback off of their marketing and make sure your marketing strategy is even better. It will also help you with your marketing as you can go after the same target audience. Make sure that they are definitely targeting the people you want to target and that their marketing is effective. There is no use in reinventing the wheel if you don't have to.

Content Analysis:

The next step is to analyze the content that is currently being produced within the niche.

Start with a simple Google search to find some of the most popular blogs within your niche. From there gather the following details:

- The name of the website
- The frequency of content being published
- The general themes of the content (e.g., tech specs, how-tos, etc.)
- The URLs of their social media profiles
- The frequency with which they distribute their email newsletter and its content (subscribe to their email newsletter)
- Traffic level estimates using SimilarWeb.com and SEMrush.com

- Look into the length of their content, the format of the content, and social shares they are using

From these core pieces of data, you can drill down into what is working for each of your competitors, the types of content that you should be looking to produce, and some of the channels where you need to invest most of your time.

Channel Analysis:

Before you set up your social media channels, you need to decide **which channels are right for you**. More importantly, you need to decide which channels will provide **the best route to your target audience**.

For example, in one of my niches of smartphone photography, because of the visual nature of my content, it made sense to drill down on social channels that would really make the most of showing off photos.

Also, since my main goal was traffic generation, I wanted to encourage a pull-through of relevant people to my blog.

After your initial analysis, you can decide which social networks to set up and which ones won't be very useful. For example, on my Smartphone Photography Academy site, I focused on Facebook, Pinterest, Instagram, Twitter, and YouTube. It wouldn't make much sense to spend a lot of time on LinkedIn since my audience is not there. However, a more business-orientated niche would definitely want to focus on LinkedIn.

Although you want to obtain as much exposure as possible, it's not always realistic to start building communities in every channel that you can; this can often have a detrimental effect, as you're not able to put enough time into each platform which results in your content becoming very disparate.

Map out the time that you can dedicate towards your social media activities. This is a simple process that takes the following into account:

- Time needed to create a content roadmap across each platform.
- Resources needed to produce any platform-specific content on each platform (e.g., resized images, custom tracking links, post descriptions, etc.).
- Any extra equipment/software that would need to be purchased or any extra skills that need to be developed.

SEO and Keyword Analysis

As you might know, this topic can be very detailed but we are only going to touch on the basics. The most important thing to understand is what keywords people are typing into the search engines to find your niche. The best tool for this is the free **Google Keyword Planning Tool**. Start by guessing on a keyword that people might use to find your niche. When you enter that word into the keyword tool, it will tell you a couple of very important things. First, it will tell you how many people search with that term each month. Second, it will list alternative keywords that are related to your keyword that may also be useful. Pick at least five keywords that will be your go to keywords for your business. Try to find keywords or phrases that have at least 100 searches per month. Remember, when I say keywords, I'm talking about keyword phrases containing three-five words. For example, "cat" is a keyword but "cat food" and "funny cat videos" are also considered keywords.

Estimating Your Budget:

Last but not least in the analyze phase is creating your budget. I usually create a separate page in my spreadsheet with budget items and their estimated costs. While you may not know all of the variables yet, you need to at least start plugging in some numbers so you can get an idea about how much it will cost to launch your online information business.

You may want to finish this book before trying to do this because you will have a much better idea of all the different components. You should list all of the channels and platforms that will need to be built for your business. Then do some research on the Internet and find out what it costs to hire qualified people to create these assets for you. Again, you can start diving in and creating these assets for yourself but don't become to overwhelmed and lost during this process. You can obtain a basic idea of what you want by playing around with some of the website creators or graphic editors just so you can tell your outsourcers what you have in mind. If I had to pick the number one outsourcer to hire, it would be a graphics designer who can help create your branding, logo, and banners for all your social media sites. Nothing says "newbie" like a poorly created logo that looks like it was created in Microsoft Word. This is an area to spend a little money in order to obtain a high-quality product.

Platform Creation

Now it's time to start creating your **branding** and **platform**. You need to create your logo and banners so you can use them in your website/blog and social media sites. Refer to Appendix B for a list of outsourcers that can do this for you.

Your platform is crucial for you to shout your message to the world. This is where all that analysis work starts to pay off as you are now ready to create your website/blog and social media platforms. I recommend starting with **Facebook**, **Twitter,** and **YouTube**. Begin by creating a new **Gmail account** using your new business name. For example, if your business is called New Beginnings then your Gmail address could be newbeginnings@gmail.com. Once you have your Gmail address, you can use it for all your other social media accounts and keep everything consistent. If you already have these social media platforms, simply move on to the next step. Before we leave this step though, let me point out that there are many, many social media sites out there and you will have to determine which ones you think will be helpful to your platform. Remember: you want to maximize your time only posting content to sites where you can reach your potential customers. For example, if New Beginnings is a financial consulting business, then maybe Facebook and Pinterest aren't the best places to find your customers. LinkedIn and Twitter might be better places to reach your customers. That's why your client analysis is so important. Don't waste time: only put your content where YOUR customers will be hanging out.

That brings us to your **website**. If you don't already have one, the next step is to create a simple but branded website with a **blog.** In my opinion, it's not that important to have a fancy website with a lot of bells and whistles. Online information businesses mostly use their website to host their blog and showcase information products. Your blog will be the location where all of your content will first be published. With the MYM system, when you are finished building your platform, you will have an automatic system that distributes your content to all of your social media sites from your blog. There are many easy website/blog creators that are mostly drag and drop and don't require any coding or HTML experience. I use **WordPress** sites myself but other good ones are **Wix** and **Squarespace**. This is an area that I suggest you don't spend too much time with. Hire a good website designer and tell them that you need a decent looking website with a blog that you can easily update with new content. You'll also want your blog posts to automatically be posted to your Facebook and Twitter accounts. Websites can be a time sucker for many small business owners. I'd much rather see you spend your time creating great content.

Creating content for your online information business is important and will take up a good portion of the time you spend on your business. The type and quality of content you create will determine how large and strong your platform will be. The bigger and stronger your platform, the more information products you will sell. It's that simple. Have you ever heard the expression "It's all about the list"? I believe that to be true; a platform that is powerful will enable you to develop the best list of buyers who desire your products. We will discuss email list building later, however, just be aware that quality content and a good email list go hand in hand.

The Peel and Pull Method Of Content Creation

Let's define quality content. An online information business is all about teaching people something they didn't know or understand. The nice thing about this type of business is we can leverage our information products to create little chunks of content for our readers to obtain their interest in our message. For example, if your online course focuses on how to meditate better, you can peel off parts of your course and create small blog posts and videos.

The whole idea of platform building is to create quality content and give it away freely on your blog and social media in the hope that people will start to know, like, and trust you enough to spend money on a more robust version of your content that is packaged in the form a book or an online course. The peel and pull method takes advantage of the structured method we use to create an online course. As you will see in other phases, by using detailed analysis and design methodologies the content you create is focused on solving your customers pains. Once that content is written and you peel or pull off portions of it for you blog posts, lead magnets and other small information products, you can rest assured that the content will be extremely valuable to your readers.

There are also many content aggregation systems out there. The two that I like are **buffer** and **post planner**. Both of these programs allow you to find content about your niche and establish scheduled delivery of the content to your social media platforms. I like to add a short paragraph at the top of the post explaining why I'm sharing this content and relating it back to my message and products. Another cool tool is **IFTTT,** which stands for If That Then This. You can program any program to work with any other program; for example, the program will forward any Facebook post to you LinkedIn account. Smart use of these tools will keep all your social media accounts updated with great content.

Another great way to create content is by using a slick little system called the **10 x 10 formula;** it was created by my friend, Mike Koenigs. In Mike's system, you answer the most frequently asked questions (FAQs) that you receive on a daily basis. These questions and answers can be placed into blog posts or videos; they make great value based content. You can also create a list of SAQs – should ask questions. These are the questions that you wish people would ask you. These are the questions that they don't know they should be asking. Again, answer the questions and add them to blog and video posts. You can create a ton of valuable content this way and it will help people to know, like, and trust you. The biggest difference between FAQs and SAQs is that an FAQ is generally what people search for online and SAQs are what set you apart and make you the expert.

Priming the Pump & Lizard Brain

You might be wondering why you have to do all this platform building and why you need to give away your best stuff before you can create your main information products and start making money. The answer is the **lizard brain.** If you've read marketing books, you would be familiar with the lizard brain. It's the part of the brain that is always trying to protect you from danger or in this case risk. In this case, the danger is the dreaded sales pitch. If your lizard brain isn't pacified with trust, it will shut you down and get you the heck away from the painful and risky sales pitch. That's why we spend so much time creating free content, so we can pacify the lizard brain with trust. Once people know, like, and trust you, and the lizard brain quiets down, their brain will take in the entire message even if there is a sales pitch at the end; their brain will be able to calmly evaluate whether or not to make a purchase. If your sales pages convey the quality of your information product to potential customers and articulate how you can solve their pain, they will open up their wallets. As you will see, when we market our information products, we don't send traffic straight to a sales page. You slowly encourage potential customers to know, like, and trust you by giving away small information products for free. The word **free** is a very powerful word. That word alone settles the lizard brain down because there is less risk with free stuff which allows us to begin a relationship with our prospects. If you follow the process laid out in this book, you will give yourself a much greater chance to succeed than if you simply create information products and attempt to sell them without lowering the perceived risk and building trust first.

Now, that you have fully analyzed yourself and your business, and created a platform, you are ready to move on to the design phase. This phase enables you to start putting all that analysis to use.

Visit http://monetizeyourmessagetoday.com/bookcta to access a bonus video on business analysis.

Design Phase

The design phase primarily focuses on the structure and sequencing of your online course. During the design phase, you will create a **design document** which includes the course outline, dates, learning objects, storyboards, resources, and notes. In the MYM system, the design phase is the most traditional instructional design process as it helps you to prepare your online course; this phase ensures the learning process is thoroughly thought through so your course and follow-up products actually solve your customers' pain. By separating this aspect from the develop phase, it allows you to focus on the learning objectives of your course without getting caught up in the nitty-gritty of putting the entire product/course together.

The design document also becomes your project plan with deadlines, milestones, and implementation details.

The Design Document

From here on out, the design document will dictate what, when, and how you create your course. This one document will detail the majority of your content and videos for your blog and information assets. That's why you need to develop it before any content is created.

After reviewing the portfolio analysis document, use a spreadsheet and give each course module a name. Detail all the information you want to cover in that module in separate rows under each module title. **This is the outline** for what you will cover in your online course. Next, create a **resources column**, a **notes column**, a **learning objectives column,** a **date column**, and a column for any other area you want to track.

It's a good idea as you build out your design document to make notes as to what resources you plan to use for each section. Remember, during the design phase, you are only putting together the shell and identifying the information that will go into the course. You can start writing some of the content here and make a note of it's location either on your hard drive or in the cloud. Create a folder structure that has each module as a folder and the various chunks of information in separate files within each folder. You can write your content in any word processor and just file them in your module folders.

The more detailed your design document is, the easier it will be to assemble and create your course and subsequent information products during the develop phase. You can also decide what type of media each chunk of information will be, i.e., text, video, or graphic.

Some chunks will be text only while others will be turned into videos or exercises in the develop phase. You can also storyboard any videos or lessons that you want to include. Simply create more columns in your design document to include these ideas or just put them in your notes section. Watch out though, as sometimes the design document can get a little crowded making it hard to find things. At this point, you can start adding dates and milestones into your design document.

Refer to Appendix C for a sample design document and folder formats.

Content Management Systems

At this point, you will need to decide what content management system (CMS) you will be using to deliver your course. The CMS is the place where your customers will complete the online course. CMS's vary in size and complexity. Some are very complex and help you to assemble your content into the final course, provide the user interface, and help you to market your course. I prefer basic CMSs that are basically just formatted WordPress or landing page website creators with templates to create membership sites. We call them membership sites because a customer needs to pay a membership fee before they can access the course. There are many great tools out there but I like **Optimize Press** and **ClickFunnels**. OptimizePress is a WordPress theme and works great. ClickFunnels is basically a landing page creator but has a membership site creation template that I also like a lot. **Kajabi and Kajabi Next** are also very good CMSs. Kajabi Next is a basic CMS and is fairly easy to use, however, there are less options regarding the look and feel of your course.

Once you decide on the CMS, you can start to develop your course shell by creating a container for each module. You can use the CMS to create all your modules in advance and give them names so all you have to do is plug in your content in the develop phase.

StoryBoard Your Videos

Most of your course content will be videos. At this point, you need to brainstorm what will be in your videos. When I say storyboard, I'm not talking about the hollywood version of literally creating a storyboard shot by shot. You merely need to outline what your video will cover and the type of video it will be. For example:

> In this module, the video will start with a talking head shot of me introducing the module and a brief overview. It will cut to a screen share video of me showing and explaining how to navigate the ABC system.

You can add anything else that seems relevant to each video. You want to add enough information so you can hand off the design document to an editor so they can put the video together.

Creating Learning Objectives

This is another very critical step in the MYM system. By creating your learning objectives before you start creating content, you give yourself the best chance to focus on solving your customers' pain. When designing and developing your content make sure it adheres to the learning objectives you have set.

The father of modern learning objectives is Benjamin Bloom who invented Bloom's Taxonomy; this is a formal classification of the different learning objectives that educators set for learners. It divides learning objectives into three domains: cognitive (mental), effective (emotional), and psychomotor (physical). Within the domains, learning at the higher levels is dependent on having attained prerequisite knowledge and skills at lower levels. The goal is to encourage educators to focus on all three domains creating a more holistic form of learning. Of the three domains, only the cognitive domain has become the standard with which to create learning objectives. Bloom created six categories in the cognitive domain. **Each category is associated with a set of verbs or cognitive processes that describe what a learner should be capable of doing after training.**

- **Knowledge/remembering:** write, list, label, name, state, define
- **Comprehension/understanding:** explain, summarize, paraphrase, describe, illustrate
- **Application/applying:** use, compute, solve, demonstrate, apply, construct
- **Analyze:** analyze, categorize, compare, contrast, separate
- **Evaluate:** judge, recommend, critique, justify
- **Synthesis:** create, design, hypothesize, invent, develop

Once you know the cognitive process that learners are expected to achieve, you're ready to write your learning objectives. Simply combine the **subject** (the learner), the **verb** from the above cognitive processes (what learners must know how to do), and the **object** or the knowledge they need to acquire.

For example: "At the end of this course, **learners** (subject) will be able to **define** (verb) the **difference between photo mode and edit mode** (object) on their smartphones cameras."

I have simplified the process and made the learning objectives a bit more consumer friendly; therefore, for our purposes, the above learning objective would look like this:

"At the end of this course you will be able to define the difference between the photo mode and edit mode on your smartphone camera."

Learning objectives are at the very core of the instructional design process. If done correctly, your leaning objectives will not only tell you what content to include in your course but what information and skill the learner must acquire to be successful. In the corporate world, they are also used to create test questions. Once you have developed the objective, you merely reform the objective into a test question. For example, from the above course objective, the test question would be: "Define the difference between photo mode and edit mode on your smartphone camera." Simple stuff, right? Well, we won't need to create test questions for our courses but you could if you so desire. In consumer-based courses, it is important that the learning objective reflects and addresses the customers' pains.

In other words, if you have created the right learning objectives in the design phase and you created content that matches the objective, your customers will be successful in achieving the desired outcomes after completing the online course. It also ensures that any information products you spin off from your online course will also be instructionally sound and solve the customer's pain or enhance their life.

First, start off by establishing the overall **course learning objectives** for your online course. Refer back to the analyze phase when you were brainstorming your business goals, specifically your client analysis. They make great course objectives. For example, if you determined that one of your customers' pains is their inability to attract good online reviews for their small business, a good course objective could be: "After taking this course, **you** will **know how to receive new reviews by creating customized postcards to send to your existing customers asking them for a review.**"

Having multiple course learning objectives is perfectly acceptable. These learning objectives will come in handy when you are marketing your course, as you will use them in your ads, landing pages, and emails to encourage people to buy your course and associated products.

After you have created your course learning objectives, go through the design document and create a learning objective statement for each module. Again, you are defining what the customer will be able to do after they complete each module of the course.

By the end of this task, you will have a complete list of what the customer can expect to accomplish and/or what pain will be solved after completing your course. See

Appendix D for more examples of good learning objectives.

Creating The Sales Offer

Now that you have created the learning objectives, you can use them to help craft the sales offer. Creating a good offer is one of the most important aspects of a successful online information business; however, knowing how to create a great one is the secret. The components of a good offer are:

*   The logistics of what your product is and how they buy it
*   Reduction and if possible, reversal of risk
*   The use of urgency and scarcity
*   The use of bonuses to overcome objections
*   Good price points and payment plans
*   The ability to sell the benefits and outcomes.

The learning objectives outline what the customer will be able to accomplish after taking the course. These are your **selling benefits and outcomes**. The beauty of this system is that you won't have to inflate the benefits in your sales offer because you know that your course content was created from the learning objectives in the design phase, and all your content was created with the objectives in mind.

For example, regarding the aforementioned photography course, the learning objective was: "At the end of this course, you will be able to recognize the difference between the photo mode and edit mode on your smartphone camera."

You would add this to your offer by focusing on the benefit that when they see a great photo opportunity they won't have to fiddle around with their smartphone camera figuring out if they are in edit mode or photo mode; this could mean the difference between getting the shot or not. In your sales offer, you could word it as follows:

"Never miss a great shot fiddling with your smartphone camera controls because you didn't know whether or not it was in shooting mode."

Basically the sales offer ensures that your course will make money providing you are addressing your customers' pain and have created a solution to solve that pain. You need to make sure you can answer these questions about your information product:

• Have you actually done the thing you are teaching and does it really work?

• Do you have proof that it works?

Unless you can market your course in a way that answers these questions, people will not buy the product. In contrast, if you can connect with potential customers, give them certainty that your course will solve their problems, they'll open their wallets and buy your product.

Customer testimonials are essential to help you answer the questions above. If you have people saying how great it was and how it solved their pain, you already have evidence that the product works. If you don't already have people who can testify for you, your online course beta test will provide them for you. Make sure to include each person's photo along with his or her quote about your product. This gives your testimonials much more credibility and provides certainty that your course will solve their pains.

You also want to reduce risk with a **money back guarantee**. If you can convince them they really don't have anything to lose by trying out your course, they will feel like there really is no reason not to at least try it out. For this, you will use the sales offer in your marketing campaigns, which will be discussed in the implement phase.

The fact that you have created your sales offer before you have created your products gives you the ability to make sure every piece of content you create adheres to your leaning objectives and sales offer. This means that your course and products will solve your customers' pains. This is the power behind the MYM system.

Develop Phase

The develop phase is where it all comes together. During the design phase, you laid out your entire online course. Now it's time to assemble everything into your final products.

Online Course Creation

Up until now, you have been playing minor league ball. It's time to step up to the big leagues. This is where you will separate yourself from 90% of your competitors. Most people don't take advantage of the massive online course market. Online courses are also the absolute best way to get your message to resonate with your customers. No other medium has as much flexibility or personalization. You will learn to provide all available media types to engage your customers. The simple fact of including audio versions of your content so your customers can listen to your content in their cars or on their portable music players and smartphones will put you way ahead of your competitors. Your customers will appreciate it and this will increase their loyalty. One of my favorite online course formats is the hybrid model, which includes both pre-recorded video content, exercises, and live webinars that allow your customers can interact with you. It's very powerful and will ensure your customers are engaged with you and your message. They will also be more likely to stay with you through your future information products and events.

First, let's define an online course. There are many definitions of what an online course is because each institution and business using them has their own slightly different interpretation. The simplest definition is "a class where both the student and instructor communicate via their computers." I would simply change the word computer to networked device. E-learning is defined as "the use of electronic technology in teaching and learning." While these definitions are pretty broad, I think you get the point.

The first step in the develop phase is to review your design document and determine what content still needs to be created. During the design phase, you identified where chunks of content were located and even created some of it. Now is the time to finish creating all your text, videos, exercises, and even the bonus content you will be offering.

Simple Text and Graphics Content

The bulk or your course will consist of videos but each module needs some form of introduction that comes in the form of text and graphics. I often create the introduction on the fly as I load my videos into the CMS. This is also a good time to upload your learning objectives. Your course objectives will appear in the introduction of your course; each module will have their own objectives. You want to make sure your customers understand what they will learn during each lesson of the course.

Video Content

This is where most of your time will be spent in creating your online course. I like to use a combination of on camera video and screen share video with voiceover. On camera video is harder to do because you need to look and sound professional. This usually entails video lights, a clean background, a teleprompter, or some kind of cue cards and a good microphone. I'm not a fan of just turning on the camera and talking off the top of your head. There is just too much room for rambling and disjointed content. You'll want to get your ideas on paper first and then either put them into a teleprompter or a PowerPoint presentation to view during recording. If you haven't used a teleprompter before, it can take a bit of getting use to. The trick is to read the words but act like you're not reading them. The audience shouldn't know that you're using a teleprompter. You really need to be enthusiastic as otherwise you give the impression that you are not really excited about your content. There is nothing worse than watching a video where it appears the speaker is really not interested in what they're saying. Record your video and save the files in your module folders on your hard drive or cloud drive. Try to save the files as industry standard video files like .mov or .avi or .mp4 or .mv4. Anything other than these and you might run into editing problems when you send the files to your video editor. That's right, I said video editor. This is another area where you should outsource the task. Video editing can be tricky and a time consuming process if you are not a professional video editor. Your videos don't have to be fancy and this shouldn't cost you a lot of money. You could even ask your editor to create a nice introduction for each video. Other than that, all you need are your videos to be edited professionally so they can be uploaded onto your video sharing site. **Youtube** is perfectly acceptable and easy to incorporate into your CMS. **Vimeo** is another good video platform to use. A lot of people use much more powerful platforms, such as **Amazon S3** servers to host their video, however, for your first online course that is not necessary. Once the videos are uploaded to your video sharing site, you can link them into your CMS under each lesson.

Screen share videos are easy with programs like **Snagit** or **Screenflow.** These programs allow you to capture your computers audio and video into a video file. They are great for showing how to do online tasks. They can be saved as standard video files and usually don't need any editing so you can upload them directly to your video sharing site for inclusion into your CMS, or you can have your video editor put multiple screen share videos into one video file. Just make sure you have a good microphone and that your audio is loud and clear with no interfering background noise.

Once you finish creating all your videos and uploading them to your CMS, you are ready to add your exercises and bonus content. Most of the time, your exercises will be in the form of PDF files that you created in Word and converted to PDF format. The most popular word processors have this feature. You will need to upload your PDF files onto a server so they can be linked to your CMS. Some CMSs make this easy and let you upload files directly to the CMS. Kajabi Next and Clickfunnels allow you to do this. If you are using OptimizePress, you can upload the files to the server where your WordPress is hosted. You can even use a cloud based storage service, such as **Dropbox** or **Google Docs** to house your PDF files. Once they are on a server, you can create links to them in your CMS so a user can download the files.

Your bonus content can be anything from special videos or additional PDF files which they can download. Just make sure to have this content ready to access before you launch your product. You could also offer previously recorded webinars on relevant topics. Be sure your bonuses are directly related to your message and are not just a hodgepodge of material or courses.

Live Webinars

If you are using a hybrid model with pre-recorded videos and live webinars then you will need to purchase a webinar system. The two I recommend are **GoToWebinar** and **WebinarJam Studio**. Both of these systems allow you to schedule, invite, and deliver live webinars. Although webinars are straight forward, you will want to run through a couple of test webinars before you do one live with your customers. Not only do webinars need to be configured properly but becoming comfortable with the user interface is important because you don't want to be fumbling with the technology when you should be delivering quality content to your customers.

As previously mentioned, I like to have at least a week in-between live webinars for a multiple week course so your customers have a chance to complete assignments and test the theories and techniques they are learning. Some courses won't have any assignments and you can just deliver your live webinars at anytime; your customers can either attend them live or view the recorded webinars at anytime.

Community

Another great bonus is to include a place that your customers can interact with you and other students during and after the course. **Facebook Private Groups** are ideal for this. After you create your private group, include the link to the sign up page in your welcome email once customers have signed up. Only do this if you or another person on your team plan to monitor it. This is a place where customers will sing your praises if they love your content and also sling the mud if they don't. You want to not only be available to answer questions but to monitor any unruly behavior that might pop-up on the forum.

Course Access

You will learn how to setup your sales pages and credit card payments in the implement phase. At this point just make sure you link a person's payment to the access for your course. OptimizePress and ClickFunnels have this function built in. You just connect your payment processor with them and once a person pays for the course they will be sent an email with their own username and password. Some systems will allow the user to create their own username and password. Consult your website outsourcer to set this up for you or contact the CMS or payment process for directions.

At this point, you need to publish the course, test the access, and have some people run through the entire purchase and access process to make sure it works smoothly.

Marketing Funnel Content

In the implement phase, you will also create your marketing funnel. As you will learn, the marketing funnel is based on generating traffic to a free information product in exchange for email addresses. It's now time to create the information products that will encourage people to know, like, and trust you so they will purchase your online course.

The Lead Magnet

A lead magnet is defined as a mechanism that will attract (magnet) leads (email address). As previously mentioned, this works well if you have your online course created or your design document finished. The idea is to peel off a part of your online course to use as your lead magnet. The key is to make sure that you give value to your customers. This will be just a taste of what you have to offer in your online course. For example, if your business is about photography and your online course is on how to use your smartphone to take great photos, you could peel off a small portion of that course and create a lead magnet that is a PDF worksheet of the best photo editing apps available on both iPhone's and Android phones. This is something you will be including and expanding on in your online course; however, this small PDF file, given away for free, will add value to people who are interested in smartphone photography. The real question is: will they find enough value in your lead magnet to hand over their email address? Don't under estimate this process. Today, people take care of their email addresses. Most people are sick of spam and know if they give out their email address there is a chance they will receive more spam in their inbox. The key is to create something that is of such high value that it overcomes their hesitancy to not share their email address. This is still a viable way to generate leads. You will receive email address if your lead magnet has valuable information in it, and if you can convince people that it will solve one of their problems. We will discuss how to market your lead magnet and why targeting people who are more likely to value your content is so important. That's why I emphasize the analyze phase and in particular your **client analysis.** If you know your clients inside and out, it will be much easier to create something they value and target them with your marketing.

There are generally four main types of **lead magnets**. The first one is a **PDF downloadable file**. This can be the easiest lead magnet to create, however, make sure it looks very professional. There are so many people out there trying to obtain people's email addresses and there is a lot of crap out there. Make sure your one or two page PDF file is professionally done and contains good graphics. Unless you are a professional graphic artist, you should hire a graphic artist to lay out the pages for you. Of course you want it to contain your logo, branding, contact formation, and social media sites. The second type of lead magnet is a **video**. This can be any type of video but your main purpose it to share something with your audience that will add value to their life. The type of video can be anything from a video of you talking to your audience or a screen share video with your voiceover. It doesn't really matter as long as it's moderately professional looking. People are fairly forgiving in what the video looks like as long as the sound quality is good. Make sure you have a good microphone when you are recording your voiceover. If you want to create a video lead magnet, follow these tips:

1. Any fairly new smartphone will shoot high quality video if you put enough light on your face. Standing or sitting by a window will give you the best light quality. If you use indoor house lights and lamps, your videos will be on the yellow/orange side but generally the video will still look good.
2. Buy a lapel microphone that can connect directly to your smartphone for good audio.
3. Put your smartphone on a tripod so you're not holding it, otherwise the vide will appear shaky. You may need an inexpensive smartphone holder/adapter that allows you to connect it to a tripod.

The next lead magnet type is my favorite. It is the combination of a **PDF downloadable file and a video**. The PDF can include the exact same content as the video or additional information to complement the video. Even though people love to watch videos, they also appreciate being able take something away and save it on their hard drive for later viewing. The following lead magnet is probably the most complicated: a **live webinar**. However, it can be an extremely effective way to attain email addresses. This works best when you are giving away great content for free or selling something at the end of the webinar. If you already have a product to sell, a webinar is a great option for your lead magnet. You will receive many new email addresses as well as some sales as you market the free lead magnet webinar. Webinars can be tricky to pull off, so if you haven't delivered a live webinar before, I'd start with one of the other lead magnet types. After using these four main types of lead magnets, you can really use your imagination to come up with other lead magnet types. For example, you could record an audio file and offer that as a download. You could even produce a series of emails that convey your free message. Anything is game as long as it meets the lead magnet definition of giving away really good content that will add value to a person's life in exchange for their email address. Don't skimp on this. Give away your best stuff - it will pay off in the end. Don't think that by giving away your best stuff that no one will want to buy your products. The opposite is true. If people like your free content, they will want more of that good stuff and will be willing to pay for it. You will learn exactly how to deliver your lead magnet during the implement phase. Basically, you will need to upload it to a host server and email the link to clients so they can download or view the content.

The Tripwire Product

A tripwire is defined as a product that is packed with great value added content. It is a small part of your online course that is inexpensive for the consumer, usually between $20-$100. The idea is to create a valuable product that doesn't cost very much in order to lower the barrier to a sale. This "primes the pump" if you will. Once someone has purchased something from you, they are more likely to purchase from you again. Sticking with my mobile photography example, the tripwire could be a mini course that has three-five videos and three-five PDF downloads and costs $35. If people have downloaded your free lead magnet and like it, they may be willing to pay $35 for another product, as long as it's perceived value is even higher than the lead magnet. Now that people have your lead magnet and tripwire information products, they are more likely to purchase your next product. The trick is to ensure that the cost difference between the two products is not too high. For example, if your tripwire costs $35, then your next product should be around $97-$150. The key is to not have your up-sells priced to high or most people won't buy them.

This is also why I like to separate my launches: for example, I separate information product launches from an online course launch that can cost anywhere between $250 to over $1000. If I tried to sell my online course as an up-sell from a $20 product, people wouldn't be ready to make that big of a leap in price.

As for types of tripwires, it's pretty much the same as the lead magnet but mini online courses work best, as they are perceived as having high value; therefore, you can charge more. Use the peel and pull method and peel off a small part of your online course for your tripwire. In the Implement phase, we will discuss the importance of creating convincing Facebook ads and landing pages, as well as sending multiple emails to those who have at least opted into your email list, as this will encourage them to purchase your tripwire.

Visit http://monetizeyourmessagetoday.com/bookcta to access the bonus videos and exercises.

Implement Phase

You will be introduced to three launch types: **the product launch**, **beta launch,** and **online course launch**. Where you are at in terms of your business will determine which launch you will use. For example, if you already have products to sell, such as a book, a product launch might make sense. A product launch usually includes a free lead magnet given away in exchange for email addresses and an up-sell to a low- or medium-priced information product.

The implement phase is the money phase. This is when you put all of your hard work out there for consumption. Even though we'll cover the product launch first, there is no hard and fast rule that says you can't jump directly into a beta launch or an online course launch. It depends on your situation: you might have a fairly established platform and a published book and therefore are keen to launch your online course. If you are starting from scratch

- with no products or content - then you might want to build up your business slowly by offering a couple of low-priced products before diving into an online course. However, it is still a good idea to create your design document, which details your online course before you create any other products. A main tenant of the MYM system is using a structured training methodology to create the highest quality products possible. Following the design phase process ensures you will create a structurally sound information product that will add great value to your customers and solve their problems.

The main part of any launch is marketing. It's hard to believe but your idea contributes to only 10% of being successful with your information business. Remember: marketing amounts to 90% of creating a successful online information business. You need to find a way to attract the right people to your marketing funnel so they will buy from you. We will cover successful Internet marketing methods that result in streams of people buying and consuming your products.

The Marketing Funnel

Regardless of which launch you will employ, you need a marketing funnel. One of the main reasons you spent so much time analyzing, designing, and developing is so that you can create a marketing funnel. A funnel uses multiple products to engage and continue to move people through it. The lead magnet is the first information product you will market. As mentioned before, it is designed to acquire email addresses and push people toward the next product in the funnel, which is the low-priced tripwire product. Once people buy the tripwire product, the funnel pushes them along to your main online course. The funnel will also catch anyone who doesn't purchase, as it will attempt to re-engage them via emails.

The system is flexible enough that you can create and market your lead magnet and tripwire separately from your online course. You might want to see how engaged your audience is before designing and creating your online course. If you can't find anyone to buy your tripwire, chances are they won't buy your online course either. This gives you a chance to redo your target audience or your lead magnet and tripwire products. This where marketing analysis is important - so let's dive into marketing.

What's a Landing Page?

A landing page is a traditional Internet marketing webpage that has one job – to convert. This is where you use the information that you created in your sales offer during the design phase.

You will create a single web page designed to entice visitors to give you their email addresses in return for valuable free content. The main job of the landing page is to explain what the visitor will receive if they enter their email address. This can be words and graphics or a video. I personally like to have a video on my landing pages because I can usually present more information and offer a sneak peak of what they will be receiving. Use your sales offer content in your text and video. Below the text or video will be what's called an opt-in box. This is the area where the viewer will type in their email address. It should be large and straightforward to use. Some people collect the viewer's name and email but I prefer to make the barrier to obtaining their email very small, so I simply ask for their email address. Once you have their email address, you can ask for their name if you want to send them personalized emails. You can host a landing page by creating a single page on your website; there are some online programs that focus on creating great looking landing pages and have many templates to choose from. They are also great because you can use them to create your entire sales funnel. After someone has entered their email address and clicked the submit button, the system will guide them to a thank you page. The thank you page that you create is actually a sales page for your tripwire. After you have thanked them and told them their free product will be accessible via an email, you start selling your tripwire product. These landing page creators are also useful for easily adding a merchant account vender to your page so you can accept credit card payments. A few examples are **ClickFunnels** and **LeadPages.** Both have many other functionalities that will be useful for your business.

Next, we will discuss an email marketing strategy that also uses the content from your sales offer; this will be the heart of your marketing strategy.

Email, Auto-responders, and Sequences

With the advent of the email auto-responder, email marketing has taken off with no end in sight. Email marketing is still the best way to ensure people come to know, like, and trust you so they will buy your information products. What's an auto-responder? It's simply an email system that automatically collects and distributes emails. Remember that opt-in box that you put on your landing page? Behind that opt-in box is the auto-responder code that actually collects their email address and puts it into your email list in your auto-responder software. The beautiful thing about auto-responders is that as soon as someone enters their email address into your opt-in box, they immediately receive an email from you. You pre-program an entire email sequence that your subscribers will receive days and months after they have opted in.

The first email they should receive is one which **thanks** them for giving you their email and investing time to consume your free lead magnet. It should also contain a link to download and view the material. The next email should be automatically sent to them a couple of hours later. This is an **introductory email** where you introduce yourself and your business. Be creative here. What do you want them to know about you and your business? You don't need to go overboard but this is the first chance you will have to talk to them and for them to get to know you. This is also a good time to ask them to visit your website/blog and social media sites. If they like what they've seen so far they might check out your blog or your Facebook page. That's why you need to have your social media platform ready to go. Make sure there is some good content on those sites, which encourages them to get know your business even more. One note here: after you have your auto-responder up and running with a few emails queued up, make sure you also put an opt-in box on your website for your lead magnet. I like to put a little banner opt-in box for my lead magnet on the right side of every page on my website. The more traffic you can generate the better. There are also plugins and widgets available that will pop-up a little box asking visitors to join your email list so they can stay up to date on all of your great content. Even though that is separate from your lead magnet, it gets people on your email list so you can promote your products to them.

You can also include a couple more introductory emails that go out a few days later. In these emails, you can add a link to any other free content that you have created. You need to take advantage of this time and showcase your content because they will never be more receptive than right after they give you their email address. However, be careful not to over do it or they'll get sick of you and unsubscribe from your email list. What's overboard? Send no more than two in one day or four or five in a week. Most weeks, you will only be engaging your list once or twice but during a launch phase it's good to send up to four or five in a week.

This is actually a really exciting time in your business. This is the first time that you can make money from your business. With an email list, you are in a good position to actually make money. Of course you aren't done building your business and there are still a lot of things that have to happen before someone will hand over their money to you, but this is a big milestone to celebrate. You have really done a lot of work up to this point and you should be proud of what you have created so far. While there is light at the end of the tunnel, don't take your foot off of the accelerator just yet.

Closing the Funnel

Since the lead magnet thank you page is actually part sales page for the tripwire, you need a place to send people when they are interested. That's where the tripwire **sales page** comes in. It's called a sales page because it includes a buy button that takes people to a merchant processor like **Paypal** or **Stripe** to make the purchase. Of course you want to have sales copy and another video to continue to convince people to buy your tripwire. Again, you obtain this information from your sales offer. If you are launching your online course, following through the funnel, when people buy your tripwire they will also be forwarded to a thank you page that again, thanks them and tries to sell them on your online course. As mentioned before, anytime they decide not to buy, they are dropped into an email sequence designed to sell your products. That's why it's so important to attain as many emails as you can with your lead magnet. Just to be clear: this entire system is assuming that you are starting from scratch with no email list in this niche. If you already have an email list that knows you, then you will also send them emails about your products.

As previously mentioned, you may want to only promote your lead magnet and tripwire and not your online course – in other worlds, a product launch. If that's the case, your funnel will end after the tripwire sales page. We haven't covered traffic yet, but if you're not promoting your online course, then let the campaign run for awhile until you are either not making any more tripwire sales or not obtain any new email addresses. Once you are ready to market your online course, you can connect your online course sales page and emails to your existing funnel or create a new one, which offers a lead magnet that connects to your online course and skips your tripwire.

Traffic and Split Testing

At this point in the process you may be wondering how anyone will come to learn about your awesome lead magnet and savvy emails? Good point. We now are moving into the murky area known as **traffic**. We all know what traffic is, right? We all have spent enough time in it. This kind of traffic is similar because we want a flood of people (or traffic) to come rushing to our landing page so they can give us their email address and receive our awesome free lead magnet. Traffic is just a marketing term used to describe how to attract people to your website, social media sites, and lead magnets.

There are many sources of traffic. You can obtain it from search engines like Google if your content has what's called high search engine optimization (SEO) value. People give Google thousands of dollars to make sure their content shows up at the top of Google searches. There are many traffic sources that businesses use to attract people, however, we will focus on paid Facebook ad traffic for now. We'll touch on a few other traffic sources when we talk about marketing your online course, but for now Facebook ads are the most reliable and cost effective traffic source to ensure people see your landing page and hand over their email address for your lead magnet.

Facebook ad marketing can be complex and confusing; we will discuss the basics so you can generate some traffic to your landing page. There are many books and online courses that deal specifically with Facebook ad marketing that may be useful if you really wish to master Facebook marketing. I believe, at this time, Facebook marketing is most cost effective and efficient because no other traffic source can target the kind of people that will most likely click your ad and sign up for your free lead magnet.

Facebook Ads

Most online information businesses will do well with a Facebook page and some good Facebook ads. Some niches that are B2B may not, as most of their potential customers will be hanging out on LinkedIn. However, for the rest of you, Facebook will be your friend. The reason that Facebook advertising is so good is that Facebook knows a lot about us. We tell Facebook about everything that is going on in our lives and what we like and don't like. This plethora of personal information allows marketers to target ads only to people who are more inclined to like our stuff. If we do this right, we won't have to waste people's time with ads that don't relate to them. No matter what you personally believe about Facebook ads showing up in your newsfeed, Facebook ads are a great way to disseminate information to people who will love your stuff.

Facebook ads work as an auction, much like Google Adwords. This means that the laws of supply and demand are at work here. With Google Adwords, some keywords will cost more per click than others. Facebook targets people and some people, strangely enough, cost more than others to reach. In Adwords, certain keywords deliver more sales to advertisers, which increases bidding competition. The same thing applies to different audience segments on Facebook. The key to low cost per click (CPC) is finding the right people to target with your ads. This is mostly accomplished by selecting the right Facebook interests in the Facebook Ads Manager. Facebook groups people into interests based on what they like. For example, if you like photography, you might like the basic photography interest and probably a few photography Facebook pages like Popular Photography and Photography week. This is how Facebook knows what you like and it allows us to target people who like photography. When creating an ad in Facebook, you search for interests based on your niche and keywords.

So finding the "right" interests is your ability to find the interests that closely match an audience that will be attracted to your message.

If you did a good job of identifying your target customers and what their pain is during the client analysis phase, then you will be able to create effective Facebook ads.

Again, I'm not going to go into detail about how to create a Facebook ad, but let me give you a few pointers to get you started. This is probably the first time anybody will see anything about you, so be sure that it is good. Your ads do not need to include your branding, as it's actually more important to catch their attention with good images and copy; your branding should appear on your landing page. You may have heard some marketers suggest that you put crazy pictures of women, babies, or puppies to grab people's attention. I am not a fan of this approach; I like good quality images that portray what your lead magnet is about or images which portray customers' pain. Going back to the photography example, a good image of someone taking a picture with a phone would work great. Just make sure it's a good quality image. In fact, I like to use Facebook's free image library - you can find this in the ads manager. You may have also heard of the Facebook Power Editor. It's a Google Chrome (only) plugin that gives you a bit more functionality than the standard Facebook Ads Manager. It's fine if you have experience using it and like it, but I don't think it is necessary to create quality Facebook ads. I find it cluttered and not intuitive to use; I prefer using the standard Facebook Ads Manager.

The first thing to understand is that currently, Facebook has three layers for categorizing your ads. All ads are housed in a campaign. A campaign can have many ad sets under it and ad sets can have many ads under it. This allows you to group your ad sets into different campaigns that may describe the type of campaign you are creating. For example, you could have one campaign called lead magnet and another for a tripwire product. This is useful so you don't get different projects mixed up. Ad sets are just another grouping of ads available. For example, under your lead magnet campaign you could have multiple ad sets that describe the types of ads it contains. For example, you might have one ad set which contains ads that have a picture of a girl, and other ads with a picture of a guy. This is actually a good practice called **split testing**. You can track which ad does better for you: the one with picture of the woman or the one with the guy. Once you determine which one is doing better, you can cancel the other and just focus on the successful ad. You can also split test a bunch of other parameters so it's best to experiment with different types of split tests. Another example would be to have an ad set with multiple ads that target different interests or different budgets. There are many options to experiment with.

For a landing page type of ad, you will select "send people to your website" for the ad type and put in the URL of your landing page. Again, you can experiment and learn about the different ad types, but for now we'll only focus on encouraging people to click your ad and visit your landing page. It may ask you for a conversion pixel and it's usually a good idea to use one; however, this issue will not be discussed in much detail in this book. Stay tuned to my website for specific training that will cover using Facebook ads to sell information products.

You can now select what age group you want to target with your ad. I usually put 18-65 which is the default. I send it to both men and women and that's the only demographics that I use. There are hundreds of other demographics that Facebook has available, but we don't need to worry about that now. You can also select the specific language you want to target, but for now you can leave it blank and it will default to the language where you're located.

Next comes the most important field in Facebook marketing: the **interest field**. This is where you will focus on targeting your ads to the people who are most likely to click on your ads. All that hard work you did in the analyze phase is going to pay off here.

Start by adding your niche into the interest box. For my Smartphone Photography business, I started with "smartphone photography" and found nothing. I then typed "mobile photography" and Facebook found it. I then started entering more niche related items to find as many niche related interests as I could. I found three more interests related to "iPhone photography." I then began entering photo apps and I was able to add about five more app related interests. I finally came up with a comprehensive list of interests: camera phone lenses, iPhone art photography, mobile photography, Vine, Camera phone, iPhone photo day, mobile photo, Flickr, iPhone photography, Adobe Photoshop Express,

Instagram, Pinterest, iPhoneography magazine, Snapchat, EyeEm, IPhoneography, olloclip, Pinterest page app, and vsco. With all of these interests selected, Facebook said there was a potential audience of 54 million people. Now when I ran my ad it said it would run it to only about 5000 people. Facebook figures out how many people to actually run the ad to based on a whole host of factors; however, it is largely based on your budget and how competitive those interests are. Again, find your favorite Facebook training source to dive into the details of ad creation.

The critical thing to understand as you are getting started is to ensure you can pick interests that will lead you to people who will like and click on your ad. Facebook will charge you less and you'll have more leads. This is where most people fail, and then wonder why their ads aren't working. There are other factors, such as the image you use or the quality of your copy. Again, make sure that your image is eye catching but related to your niche. Also, make sure your ad copy is compelling and grabs their attention by pointing out some pain people in this niche may experience; you can encourage them to click on your ad by showing them that you can help them. Use your sales offer to create compelling ads.

Ad Analysis & Performance

Now that you have created your lead magnet, landing page, and tripwire, and ran some traffic to it, you'll want to analyze the data and figure out if your campaign was successful or not. This first campaign is called the **control campaign**. You need to determine if it was profitable or not, or in this case, whether it generated enough email address. If it wasn't profitable or if you didn't receive many email addresses, you'll want to figure out why. There are many factors that will cause a campaign to either succeed or fail; you may just need to tweak a few things here and there and try again, or you may need to start over.

Profit

This first measure we want to look at is profit. It is calculated with revenues, cost of goods sold, and marketing costs (ad spend). For example, if your ad campaign cost $300 and generated $500 in revenues through the sale of your coffee table book, and the book cost $6 to create and ship and you sold 10 of them for a total costs of goods sold of $60, the formula would look this: $500 - $60 - $300 = $140 profit.

ROI - Return On Investment

From there we can create our return on investment or ROI. This is a measure of gain based on what it cost to market your product. The formula is: profit / ad spend X 100. Using the example above, you have $140 / 300 x 100 = 47%. This is not fantastic but it is not bad considering a 10% ROI in the stock market is considered good.

EPC - Earning Per Click

Now we'll get a bit more granular and look at traffic only statistics. The first thing you need to know is your earnings per click (EPC): this measures how much profit a click generates in a given campaign. The formula looks like this: profit / clicks = EPC For example, if you generated $1000 on 900 clicks, your EPC would be $1.11. 1000 / 900 = 1.11. So, for every click you receive on your ad (or email, blog, affiliate, etc.), you generate $1.11. With that information, you can go for 10,000 clicks next time and earn $11,100.

CPC – Cost Per Click

Cost per click (CPC) is the amount of money it costs you when a visitor sees an ad displayed by Facebook and clicks on it. Facebook will display CPC on the main ad dashboard. It's important to know the CPC because you want to compare it with your EPC to see the effectiveness of your campaign and determine if you are acquiring a positive or negative ROI and profit. Using the above example, if your EPC is $1.11 then you want your CPC to be well under that, right? If it's not, then you are in the negative ROI and will need to do something with your ads to fix this.

SLO – Self-liquidating Offer

An SLO is a campaign that breaks even after marketing expenses are taken into account in the hopes of profiting on the back end of your campaign at a later date. It's a way to acquire a lead at no cost. An SLO allows your front end to pay for your marketing while you profit on the back end. Sometimes it's a good idea to start off with an SLO and profit later. If you happen to profit on the front end, well, that's a bonus. For example, if your CPC = $1.00 and your EPC = $1.00, then you broke even but you acquired a lead. This lead will be valuable down the road; that is an SLO.

CTR – Click Through Rate

CTR is a way of measuring the success of an online ad campaign for a particular website or landing page as well as the effectiveness of an email campaign by the numbers of user that clicked on a specific link or ad. Obviously the higher the CTR, the better. You want people to be clicking the link in your ad or email to see your offer. Facebook gives this statistic in the ads main dashboard; most auto-responders also display this statistic.

The point of the above exercises is to determine if your marketing funnel is effective, and if not, where it is failing. Each component of the funnel is critical to the success of the campaign. If any one area is falling short, the entire campaign will suffer. For example, if you have an ad that contains a good image and professional copy, and you receive a lot of click throughs to your landing page, then you know your Facebook ad is in good shape. However, if the people visiting your landing page do not opt in and give you their email address, then the entire campaign failed because the offer on your landing page was not convincing enough. You would want to start split testing different versions of your landing page and see if one of the versions starts converting. Next, if people are giving you their email address and consuming your lead magnet but not buying your tripwire, then you need to work on either the tripwire product itself or the tripwire sales page.

For all three launch types: product, beta, or online course,use the traffic generating method described above.

If you are using the MYM system to only create a content marketing strategy, then you can eliminate the tripwire and sales pages in the funnel. Everything else should work just the same.

The Beta Launch – Test Your Online Course

The marketing funnel for launching an online course is basically the same as your product launch except with an online course, you need to beta test it with a small group of people so you can find out what works and what doesn't work. If you can find enough people on your own (friends, colleges, social media groups) to participate in your beta test, then you may not have to create an entire marketing funnel; however, if you are unable to do so, create a marketing funnel as outlined above and start sending it traffic.

Should you charge to attend the beta test? The answer is: probably. You know you have a good course because you have followed a structured method of creating great learning objectives and modules that aim to solve your customers' pain. The people who attend your beta test course believe it has great value, so you should charge something. I like to lower the price by at least 50% of the full course; also, I promise them they'll receive the full course, at no extra charge, when it comes out and more of my personal time than would otherwise be available during the course. The only reason that you wouldn't charge is if the course is incomplete and you want to get a couple of people in a room (or on a webinar) and run through the design document and work through some of your rough draft content and exercises. This might be a good idea if you are having trouble deciding on what content you want in the course, or if you don't know if your concepts will work or not. Other than that, I strongly suggest you charge for your beta test. If you don't, you'll have trouble keeping their focus and motivation throughout the beta course since they don't have any skin in the game.

The only difference from the product launch is that you need to connect your sales page and merchant account to your CMS so it can create a separate account for each user, and deliver them a username and password.

Delivering Your Beta Test

Now that you have your beta test course ready to go, make sure you follow the course access process in the develop phase so people can access your course.

Document Your Testimonials

Before you begin your beta test, you need to document where your beta test customers are starting from so you can measure where they end up after finishing your course. These stories will become the testimonials for your main online course launch. As previously mentioned, testimonials are a critical feature of your sales offer. If you are using their quotes, which convey how much your course has helped them, be sure to include their photo. You might even want to record a few video testimonials that you can add to your sales pages.

Delivery

At this point, you have your customers enrolled in your beta test course and you are ready to deliver it. The type of course you have set up will dictate what happens next.

If your course is entirely video and text based, then all you have to do is allow your customers take the course. You can make all the modules available to them or you can "drip" the content out to them week by week. This option is available in most CMSs. This is usually a good idea, as you can control the pace of delivery. As mentioned in the develop phase, one of the best delivery methods of online courses is the hybrid model where you have pre-recorded content combined with live webinar sessions. Customers can consume the pre-recorded videos and exercises before participating in a live webinar where they can ask questions. You can then offer a short overview of the next module. You can continue with this format throughout the entire course. The benefit to this method is that you can record the live webinars and make them available to your current customers; you can also package them up for a future product or make them part of you next product offering.

Feedback

If you are "dripping" the content, it's a good idea to send and email to your customers each week asking for specific feedback on each module. Either way, make sure to ask for their feedback along the way. They know that this course is in beta and one of the expectations of beta users is to provide good feedback to make the final course even better. Refer to Appendix C for a sample feedback form you can use during your beta test.

Once your beta test is complete and you have collected your feedback, it's time to incorporate it into your final course. Once you make the final additions, subtractions, and changes, you can organize a course launch and make some real money.

Final Online Course Launch

You have come so far and worked so hard. It's finally time to - WORK HARDER! At least you are in the final stretch and there is light at the end of the tunnel. Actually this is a great milestone to have a mini celebration. You are finally ready to launch your baby to the world.

At this point, you know what to do. Launch your marketing funnel, send it some traffic, and get this party started. Spend some extra time perfecting your sales offer, which will be included in the marketing material in your funnel. Take everything you learned from your beta test and update and improve your sales offer, especially your testimonials. The only thing we will add now is a few more traffic sources and a JV/Affiliate program.

JV Partners and Affiliates

What's a JV partner? They are people who you've teamed up with on a joint venture. They can be anyone from friends to business partners who will help you sell your online course for a commission. Usually, they will email their list on your behalf and try to encourage their followers to sign up and buy your course. You want to make sure you partners have a similar audience as yours or else the message won't match and you will not succeed. Also, understand that it takes time to build up a relationship with JV partners. You never want to assume any business in your niche or related niche will want to join with you. It's usually best if you offer a reciprocal offer to email your list with their offer when you can. Ideally, you'll want to build that relationship before your launch by emailing your list for one of their products first and then requesting they do the same for you. You can also create an affiliate program where anyone who wants to can sign up to become an affiliate of your products. There are many good online affiliate systems that will automate this for you. **LeadDyno** integrates with Clickfunnels and Stripe - this is one that I've used. **Nancast** is another good JV and affiliate tracker; it is also a full shopping cart. These programs make it easy to track and pay your JV partners and affiliates.

Webinars

One of the best ways to launch any product, but most especially an online course, is to conduct a live webinar. There is no better method to convince someone to buy your course then if you live sell it to them. If you can't physically be with them while your selling (such as being on a stage), then a live webinar is the next best thing. Participants can see your presentation and hear you talk through the presentation. Most webinars just show the presenters screen as they present value based content and their sales offer at the end.

A lot of times you can work out a deal with your JV partners to have a specific webinar just for the people on their list. This is a great sales technique because your JV partner has already built up trust with their audience and if they endorse your product live on a webinar, your chance of making a sale increases. Again, there are some great webinar systems out there. One of the oldest is **GoToWebinar** but another really good webinar system and the one I use is: **WebinarJam Studio**. These systems can integrate with your auto-responder email system to automate invitations and even track who actually attended the webinar, or who signed up but didn't attend so you can send them an email with the replay.

Webinars should add value to anyone who attends whether or not they buy your product. The same concept that applies to your lead magnet applies here. As previously mentioned, webinars make great lead magnets as they provide value to the participants and are live sales videos, which encourage people to buy your online course. Make sure that you have a very good presentation that includes your killer sales offer that you can provide at the end of the webinar. Many marketers like to create a special landing page just for live webinars so you can send participants directly to it and make sales.

Three Part Video Launch

Another great launch strategy is to create a three or four part video series. These video series offer great value to the viewer and always have an underlying sales message. It's basically the sales offer on steroids. Just as we discussed in the design phase, you must connect with potential customers and give them certainty that your course will solve their problem.

During the first video, the formula is to introduce yourself and the problems or pains that people in that niche experience. You can tell people that you experienced the same problem until you figured out the magic method that solved the problem, and now they too can access the magic method. In video two and three, you expand on offering good information along with your basic sales message and testimonials. In the final video, you completely unveil your course, bonuses, how much it costs, and how they can access it.

After you launch your course and pay your affiliates, you then start the delivery of the course. It is a good idea to make module one content available to anyone who buys your course so they can get started right away.

You'll also want to make sure you have programed a series of emails that will automatically be sent out welcoming them to the course and outlining what they can expect in the next coming weeks or months.

Don't forget to add a sign up link in your welcome emails for your private Facebook group if you choose to include one.

Course Delivery

From there, you deliver your course and look forward to celebrating with a massive party after your first online course has ended. You can also take a nap. However, you're not quite done yet. Let's move on to the last phase in the MYM system.

Visit http://monetizeyourmessagetoday.com/bookcta to access the bonus videos and exercises.

Evaluate Phase

Most people don't usually perform the concepts in this phase. They are generally so tired after their course launch and delivery that they need a rest. After your well-deserved rest, it's vital to spend some time evaluating your business. At this point, you should have an idea about what your next move will be given you outlined a two-year plan for your business during the analyze phase.

Review Your Business

Now it's time to look back and figure out what went right, what went wrong, and where you might want to adjust your two-year plan. It's also a good time to look back at your life perspective that was captured in the analyze phase. Has anything changed? Has your business progressed as you had hoped? Did you accomplish the things you wanted and did you spend your time productively? Did you make the kind of money you wanted? And most importantly, did you enjoy the journey? This is a great time to reflect on all those questions and create some new goals and plans for the next steps in your business. Are you ready for live events or do you want to create more online courses or products?

Soliciting Feedback

One of your first steps should be to set up a time to request feedback from your course participants after they have completed the course and put into practice what they learned. I would say three to six months out from the end of your course delivery is a good time to obtain feedback. You can also solicit and monitor feedback on your social media sites and your Facebook private group if you created one. With the pace of change in this industry, improving your course is necessary to remain relevant. I like to update my course at least once a year with fresh content as well as arrange a re-launch. Alternatively, you can mothball that course and create a new one. Make sure you leave the content where it is so your customers can continue to access it. If your course is good, people will want to look over it again to refresh their knowledge.

This is also a great time to attain testimonials for version 2.0 of your course. Don't forget to create a couple of video testimonials too.

Evergreen Sales Funnel

Depending on the format of your course, you may be able to open the course to anyone who wants take it at any time. This entails creating an evergreen sales funnel and access to your course. This works great for courses that do not contain any live interaction. Even if you included live webinars during your launch, you can add the recorded webinars and turn it into an evergreen course. This is where you can make money in your sleep, as people will be buying and taking your course 24 hours a day, 7 days a week.

Setup Your Newsletter and Email Sequence

The next step is to make sure your email sequence is set up to fuel your evergreen marketing funnel. During the implement phase, you set up the front end of your email sequences. You created your introduction sequence and your product sales sequence. Now it's time to create your monthly newsletter sequence and find a way to re-engage people who haven't bought anything from you. Since you developed a two-year business plan, you know what your next product or products will be; consequently, you'll want to market those products to your current list when they are ready to be launched. This is all created in your auto-responder software. First, create a newsletter template so you can edit the template each month and distribute it to your entire list. The newsletter doesn't need to be fancy; it can perhaps mention your last few blog posts. The newsletter is a way to remind those on your list about your business so they don't forget about you. As you create new products, you can create a new sequence to send to your existing list. You'll also be creating a brand new marketing funnel for the new product with your introduction sequence and a new product sales sequence for the new people that will join your list.

Finally, you need to weed out the people on your list that have never bought anything from you. If your auto-responder has a way of recording who has bought from you and who hasn't, you can delete the ones that haven't bought anything from you for over the past year or two. Alternatively, you can export them to a different email auto-responder system and email them once a quarter and hope they re-engage with you. The reason you want to remove non-buyers from your main list is that the email providers can flag your emails as non-responsive and not actually give your emails a very high priority. Much like Google, if they see your emails never receive a response, they will deem it junk and not give it any priority. Therefore, it is important to weed out anyone who hasn't responded or even opened one of your emails for over a year.

Platform Cultivation

Now that you have launched your course and all the associated content, it's time to make sure your social media platforms are continuing to grow and encouraging people to know, like, and trust you.

Depending on how automated you were able to make your platform during the analyze phase, now is the time to make sure you have a content publishing schedule and an automated way to post your blog content to your social media platforms.

Congratulations! You are now the proud owner of an online information business that was built around your life perspective and allows you to shout your message to the world. You will help many people and make money while you slumber.

Gotcha, I didn't say sleep.

If you haven't already, visit http://monetizeyourmessagetoday.com/bookcta to access the bonus videos and exercises.

Appendix A: Content Resources

*1 - Capstone Requirements Document: Global Information Grid (GIG 75 (JROCM 134-01) (Aug. 30, 2001)

* 2 Statisticbrain.com

Appendix B: Outsourcing Resources

Elance   www.elance.com
ODesk   www.odesk.com
Fiverr   www.fiverr.com
99Designs   www.99designs.com

These are websites that aggregate freelancers that you can either bid on or hire per project.

Endlessrise   www.endlessrise.com

This company is a full service, Internet marketing outsourcer.

Craigslist   www.craigslist.com

You can always look on Craigslist for freelancers who can do anything from providing full on virtual assistance to website design.

Hire My Mom www.hiremymom.com

This is a great resource for virtual assistants.

Outsource   www.outsource.com

Very wide resource for many different types of freelancers that can handle anything from SEO to website design.

Appendix C: Samples

Design Document

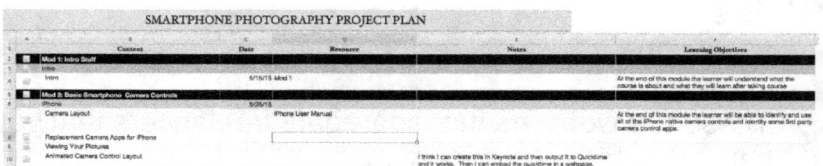

Folder Formats

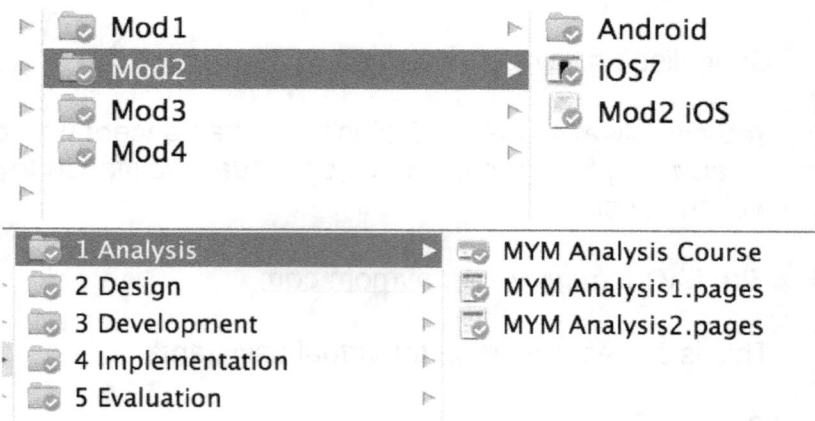

Feedback Forms

Beta Course Evaluation Questions

Course Expectations

- Rate your understanding of course expectations and assignments
- What topics were you expecting, or would have liked addressed, that were not covered?
- Did the course cover the content you were expecting? Why or why not?

Course Structure and Content

- Rate your understanding of the course course structure
- How consistent was the course content with the objectives?
- How relevant was the subject matter or course content?
- Was the content arranged in a clear and logical way?
- Did the content adequately explain the knowledge, skills and concepts it presented?
- Rate your confidence level for completing the knowledge or skill presented.
- How would you rate the amount of material covered?
- Did you utilize any links to external web sites?
- Did any of the activities help you gain a clearer understanding of the subject?
- Did the use of case studies and scenarios help you gain a clearer understanding of the content?

- Rate the following elements according to how helpful they were to your learning experience (how well these items helped you remember key information: Scenario based content, Quizzes, Exams, Games
- Rate the quality of the examples presented in the e-learning
- What part of the e-learning course did you find most useful and interesting?
- What additional material would you like presented in the course?
- Rate the availability of the instructor via email or online discussion
- I would prefer to have the instructor physically present in the same room with me
- Your opportunity to interact with other virtual students in class discussion
- Rate how isolated you felt from other students
- Rate how much you missed direct, in-person interaction with other students
- Rate your enjoyment of the course
- Rate the course workload
- What are the strengths and weaknesses of this e-learning course?

Quizzing

- Rate the relevancy of assignments, quizzes, and test
- Rate the quality of the questions asked in the quizzes
- Was there enough variety in the types of quizzes?
- Was the quiz feedback timely and relevant?
- Did the quiz feedback present new knowledge?
- Were the quizzes presented in adequate intervals?
- Did the quizzes appropriately test the material presented in the course?
- How could the exams be improved?
- Were the review sections before the quizzes useful?

- Would you prefer to have seen practice questions and to have practice questions posted before an exam?
- Did the practice questions make good learning tools?

Timing

- What was the (average) amount of time you spent on this e-learning course?
- How many hours did you spend completed activities related to the course? (Forums, chat rooms, emails, etc.)
- Did you feel the amount of time it took to complete this course was appropriate for this content?

E-Learning Pace and Navigation

- How would you rate the pace at which the e-learning course advanced?
- How would you rate the ease of navigation?
- Did the e-learning unfold in a clear direction?
- Did you understand where you had to click to move forward? If not, why not?
- Rate the e-learning access set up or LMS set up

Multimedia

- Rate the amount of multimedia (audio, video, and animation) used in the course
- Rate the quality of multimedia (audio, video, and animation) used in the course
- Rate the amount of photography used ion the course
- Rate the quality of the photography used in the course
- Rate the amount of audio track used in the course
- Rate the quality of audio used in the course
- Rate the amount of narration used in the course
- Rate the voice and quality of the narration used in this course
- Rate how satisfied you are with the narration in this course
- Did the narration add value to this e-learning module?

- Were the animations posted in the course content useful?
- How can the animations used in the course be improved?
- If you did some group work, did you enjoy working with your group?
- Rate the availability of technical support
- What was the most frustrating technical problem you encountered during the course?

Interactivity

- This e-learning course contained opportunities for interactive learning. Agree or Disagree?
- Was the interactivity were suitable for the content? Why or why not?

Visual Design

- Rate the overall aesthetic of the course content and materials
- What comments do you have about the visual design of the course?
- Rate the legibility of the text and fonts in this course
- Rate the amount of corporate branding (logos, corporate colors) used in the e-learning

Overall Experience

- Rate the technical quality of the course materials
- Rate how confident you feel about your knowledge on the subject
- List three important concepts or ideas that you learned in this course
- Identify three ways to improve this e-learning course
- Make two suggestions to improve understanding of the course content
- Would you prefer to take this course online or in the classroom?

- Based on this experience, would you take another e-learning course? Why or why not?

Learning Objective Samples

Course Learning Objectives

Upon completion of this course, you will be able to identify and use the camera controls for both iPhone and Android smartphones.

Upon completion of this course, you will understand basic photographic exposure concepts that will enable you to take better photos with your smartphone.

Module Learning Objectives

At the end of this module, the learner will understand what the course is about and what they will learn throughout course.

At the end of this module, the learner will be able to identify and use all iPhone native camera controls and identify some third party camera control apps.

At the end of this module, you will understand the basics of camera exposure and the important role it plays in terms of taking better photos.

* 9 7 8 1 5 3 0 7 4 5 6 5 4 *